# THE
# LIFE
# JOURNEY OF A
# QUAKER
# ARTIST

DOROTHEA BLOM

Pendle Hill Pamphlet 232

*About the Author*/Teacher, writer, and artist, Dorothea Blom began her career in art as a designer of batiks in the studio of a Madison Avenue shop. Later she wrote on design and color for house and garden magazines and New York City newspapers, and in the course of time co-authored nine books published by Doubleday, Barrows, and King Features. This career ended when her contemplative temperament and the artist in her converged in an event that changed her life and led to a new vocation. Since then she has focused on art as a link between inner and outer worlds, a link which can determine our relation to ourselves and to our culture. Dr. Edward Robinson of Manchester College, Oxford University, uses slides of her water-color meditations in certain of his programs on religious experience research. Many of these water colors are privately owned in the United States and abroad. The last two summers Dorothea has taught at the School of New Resources at the College of New Rochelle, New York, a pioneer venture in education which she finds one of the most exciting teaching opportunities of her life.

Request for permission to quote or to translate should be addressed to Pendle Hill Publications, Wallingford, Pennsylvania 19086.

Copyright © 1980 by Pendle Hill
ISBN 0-87574-232-7

Library of Congress catalog card number 80-80916

Printed in the United States of America by
Sowers Printing Company, Lebanon, Pennsylvania

October 1980: 3,000

OUR COVER: *The Wave,* 1978, by Dorothea Blom. Hokusai had his wave and Dorothea Blom has hers. In fact, she has painted a whole series of waves. They grew out of meditations on the first chapter of Genesis, which proclaims a creation happening now and always, both in us and in our world.

> *A life never lived before, for which there is no pattern.*
> JOACHIM OF FLORIS *(1215–1238)*

THE PAST CHANGES as I change, and even while I ponder and write these pages transformations take place. As the shape of a mountain alters when one moves to a new position, so it is with a life. There is no "objective reality," only vantage points, or different levels in inner space, from which we see and which transform what we see.

My life falls into three periods. The first twenty-five years were the hardest, a time I looked back on for many years as unmitigated depression, as a "sick" period. The second span, from my twenty-fifth year to my early forties, consisted of discovering new relations to life and learning to trust new inner landscapes and climates within the context of Quakerism. The third period extends into my present sixties, a time characterized by a process of reconciling opposites, including a reciprocity between myself and events.

## I. *A Stepchild of the Culture*

Long ago I gathered up the child that I was, embraced her — thereby discovering her core of health — and she healed and became a growing point for me. She had many secrets she shared with no one, and these secrets nourished her in spite of the withdrawn and sad exterior. As long as I, the adult, closed her out (fearful I might *be* her) she could not heal, and I could not rejoice in her secrets.

Exploring my earliest memory I find her standing in the dark at the top of the stairs looking down at a Christmas tree and a blazing fire in the fireplace. No other light is on, and no one knows she is there. Reflections of the leaping flames dance on the tree balls and tinsel. Probably she was only three.

I accept this gift she gives me and use words like mystery, enchantment, wonder, to describe it. Surely this is where my relation to the Tree of Life began, my most life-enhancing symbol for self.

Not until I was in my thirties did I realize that the little girl of three looking at her Christmas tree, like some other events of those early years, was indeed a religious or mystical experience. From Rufus Jones I learned that children have this kind of experience, but find no connection between it and their religious training. (Browning, said Rufus, makes the same observation.) Years later I recognized Buber's description of the infant in *I and Thou,* and knew it to be "the simple magic of life" I had known as a child. Finally the little girl that I was rejected and forgot those inexplicable happenings.

During pre-school years this little girl found contentment in solitary play, acting out fantasy, making dolls out of weeds. The oldest of five, she had acquired two younger sisters before beginning school. The family lived outside New York City. Both parents were career oriented, and neither had known fulfilling family experience in childhood. The little girl saw her parents somewhat as Gods on Olympus, distant but essential. In relation to others she felt as though life moved on without her. Once she told herself, "I am not part of the world. This is what it's like to be old and ready to die." Sometimes she caught glimpses of a black cloud of doom hovering near. But there was her dream world as an escape, a family of her own creation which gave her the expressive affection and closeness which in real life her parents reserved for each new baby in turn. There were a brother and sister in this dream family, and they were always her own age, growing up with her. Once she asked her mother why in some families people touched one another lovingly, but not in her family. Her mother answered, "When you *really* love someone, that isn't necessary."

As a child she had an instinctive trust of images that came to her in dreams, and was even curious rather than frightened by an occasional nightmare. One night when she was in bed an image came of a bubbling spring forming a small pond, sur-

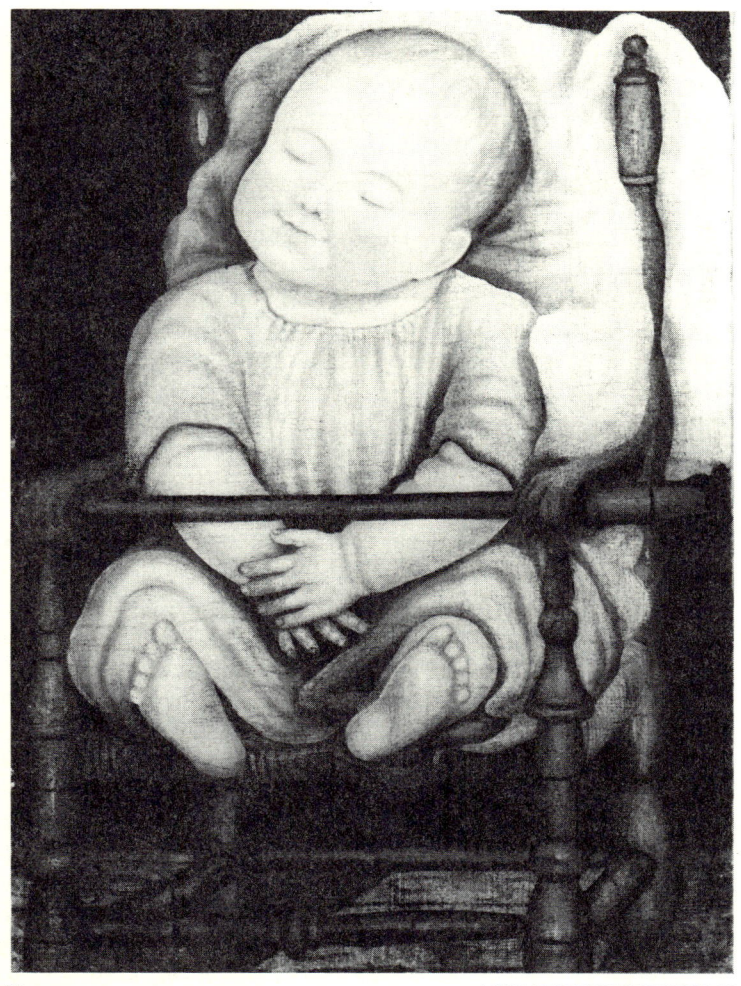

Oil on canvas

ABBY ALDRICH ROCKEFELLER
FOLK ART CENTER
WILLIAMSBURG, VIRGINIA

*BABY IN RED CHAIR, ca. 1825: artist unidentified (American). The infant soul represents the incorruptible core of innocence always present in the life journey. Even when we lose touch with it, and cannot credit its existence, it waits within us for rediscovery.*

rounded with rich plant growth. It comforted and strengthened her. So every night, for a long period, she recalled this image before going to sleep. I, the adult, name it an oasis, or a mandala.

Toward the end of the pre-school years two events stand out. First, she rejected God. She hated oatmeal, and one morning the family maid said, "You ungrateful child! Sulking over your oatmeal again while Armenian children starve to death. You ought to thank God for your cereal." Then and there this child knew she wanted nothing to do with a God so stupid as to give her the oatmeal she hated and let those who needed it starve.

The other event—the most dramatic of those early years—was her final "religious experience" of childhood. She often stayed with an aunt on a large farm. These were her happiest periods because she found life simpler playing alone in the wide expanses, talking to squirrels, and creating little dramas related to her imaginary family. Her security required that she make boundaries for herself in this seemingly endless outdoor territory, appeasing a superstition common to childhood. One day she found herself playing near one of these boundaries, a split rail gate closing off an abandoned road. As she paused to look down the road, watching it curve out of sight into the woodland, she felt the magic of the unknown. Hesitating, but unable to resist, she squeezed through the rails and trespassed into forbidden territory.

Suddenly in an unfamiliar world, she found everything intensely alive. She crept toward the curve. In the silence the snap of every twig she stepped on sounded like a clap of thunder. When she reached the curve she could see in both directions at once, deep into the mysterious woods and back to the familiar gate. She froze, unable to move in either direction. Every stone, every blade of grass, every leaf throbbed with life. Even space had a life of its own. Seized with terror, she was unsure whether her feet could tear loose from the ground she stood on. With a strength roused by panic she plunged into a run back to the gate, squeezed between the rails, and ran down the familiar road to her favorite field. There she threw herself on the ground among the tall grasses, gasping, "Never again! It must never happen again!"

So it was that, at the age of five, I lost my innocence. I lost touch then and there with that incorruptible, indestructible core of innocence which I believe to be in all human beings, whether they are in touch with it or not.

Entering school was a frightening experience for me and one I didn't get over for years. My life with my imaginary family became more absorbing, influenced by the classmates I admired from a distance. In the eyes of others I remained withdrawn, unavailable, and a great worry to my parents. I can remember my father saying, "She's such an introvert. Maybe as she gets older she'll get better." Hearing this, I assumed I had a disease. When, at the age of ten, I still couldn't read, I knew I never would, and told myself, "I'm not normal."

But soon after this a great change took place in my life. A substitute art teacher came to school for just one term. She was the first adult who accepted me for what I was, who didn't seem to share my parents' worries about me or any trace of the bored and exasperated patience of the other teachers. For the first time I found a lively satisfaction in art work, discovering in it a life line between me and the world. When the teacher left after three months I clung to her—I don't think I had ever clung to anyone before.

I don't remember feeling unhappy after she left. I do remember what it felt like, the following year, to find out that I could read and that for the first time in my life I was doing well in school. For several years my work was above average, but I grew increasingly bored and unhappy, smouldering with anger over what I considered insults to the human dignity of students who were having trouble learning. Also, my life had become one of violent conflict.

Until I was ten my dream life took precedence, and I let the world pass by. (A helpful psychiatrist whom I encountered in my late twenties said that my dream world had been my "life boat," a means of survival as I awaited the person and event that would make a difference in my life.) Now I began to find the imaginary family in competition with the world of my peers. Yet how I longed to become part of that world! This meant over-reaching, clowning, hamming. It meant withdrawing again and again into fantasy life, with a sense of helplessness at my defeat in the "real world."

A baby sister, my first love, died when I was twelve, and I felt isolated, distraught, and savagely angry: if there was a God who created this world, I could not respect him enough to unload my anger on him, so I hoarded it. This infant lived only a few weeks, but I'd dreamed of her before she was born. She seemed especially mine, and in the short time she lived she became the center of my life, a new connection with the outer world.

At the same time I was beginning to develop close friendships with girls more stable than I, usually slightly older, and capable of unusual understandings. Thus emerged one of the greatest gifts of my life—deep, mutually nurturing friendships. As I get older these special friendships are increasingly with younger people.

During my first year in high school I did enough baby-sitting to send myself to an adult art school the following summer. Returning to high school in the fall, I was exasperated with boredom, anger, and meaninglessness, and I literally did not know how to endure. When I told my father I wanted to leave school, he surprised me by saying, "All right. But you'll have to find an alternative first."

So the next morning, with my portfolio under my arm, I went to New York, looking for either a job or an art school which would give me a scholarship. I found neither, and knew in my heart I had nothing solid to offer. At the end of two days' search I remembered Walden, a very expensive private school where a friend went. Undoubtedly it was the foremost "alternative" school in New York City at that period, and it was strong in the arts. Immediately, in a state of excitement, I went there, walked into the director's office, and suggested to her that they accept me and let me pay the bills after I grew up. She listened carefully, then asked me to come back the next day.

My second visit lasted all day—interview after interview. Then the director saw me again and said: "We don't believe in letting a person your age commit herself to future debts. Our classes are limited to twelve, and with school beginning next week, we are one short in a class you could enter. We offer you a scholarship. You will be required to take English and history, plus anything else you want, and spend the rest of your time in the studio. If anything comes up which seems right for you and us, giving you an opportunity to earn part of your tuition, we'll talk about it." The next week I began commuting to Walden.

The students there were the most brilliant, articulate, and expressive peers I'd ever known. Their motivation for learning was both strange and exciting to me. In those days Walden had no examinations, no marks, and encouraged high participation in small classes. At the beginning of the year each class planned its curriculum under the guidance of the teacher. There was intense interest in social justice, and a world view. Even Communism wasn't an alarm signal. The interest in Freud was also strong, and I attended a psychology class based on his work.

One effect of this whole new environment was cultural shock and retreat into shyness. On the other hand, I acquired a self-motivation and excitement about learning that I have never lost. Also I began to explore human and social values other than the conventional ones I'd always questioned. I began to see life on this planet as process, and hoped I could take part in this process. Walden helped prepare me for Quakerism, and Walden never knew how much it did for the quiet, elusive student I was.

The following year Walden exchanged art teachers with a school in Vienna, and I was asked if I'd like to help the visiting teacher find her way around New York, and assist her in the studio. I said yes. This opened up the richest friendship of my young years. The art work I did with her was beyond anything

I'd ever done before—or after, until middle age. I even won a contest for a program cover for Carnegie Hall.

She insisted on my working to music. In recent years—through the influence of a Pendle Hill student of mine—I often move to music to experience with my body a meditation theme I'm focusing on in some art medium.

The year after leaving Walden I was employed in a batik business producing freehand designs in dress lengths and other paraphernalia for an expensive Madison Avenue shop, and living in a residence run for artists. On a modest scale, I seemed to have everything important to me: independence, a job as an artist on a livable salary (with two raises in six months), a few friends, time to paint, unlimited chances to go to museums and art galleries, take courses, attend the Civic Repertory at 50¢ a throw, and eat in ethnic restaurants!

But in spite of all this, something was missing. I could remember one Sunday School teacher I once had who gave me a feeling that there was something real and important about religion. I began shopping around. After a brief flirtation with the Oxford Movement (Moral Rearmament), I finally landed in the Community Church at Town Hall. In art circles of the time religion tended to be discredited because of the conventionality of churches in general, and my two close friends were indulgently amused by my interest in religion. I remember a couple of years earlier passing a Quaker Meeting in the car with my father and saying, "Sometime I'd like to go there and see what it's like." He said, "Please don't. You are too introverted already, and it will only make you worse." I must have suspected he was right, because it was several years before I walked into that Meeting House.

I appreciated my life, and considered myself extremely lucky, for this was the first year of the Depression. But I was having severe attacks of my own depression. Though the art world seemed normal to me, it didn't make me feel better. I'd assumed that either the culture or I must be sick: sometimes it was the culture, and now it seemed to be me. I was nineteen years old.

By spring I had left my job, and stayed home to spend the summer gardening. In the fall I became a student of Occupational Therapy in a mental hospital, but was soon transferred to the status of patient. At the point when doctors wanted to send me to a State Hospital for two years, my father rebelled. I can still hear him saying, "I will not have her spend the best years of her life in a mental hospital!"

Instead, he took me home, though the doctor had warned him that I'd probably take my life. Once home, he told me what the doctor said, and made me promise I wouldn't kill myself. I think for me this promise was a security guarantee: I don't think I was suicidal, and in any case I did not want to die. The doctor let my father take me home on condition that he find a nurse-companion to be with me. My father tried but never found the right person, so *he* became my nurse-companion. His offices were at home then, making this practical.

I used to think of the following five years as a period of unspeakable suffering. There seemed an almost invisible black veil between me and the future. Time spent with a callow young interne at the out-patient wing of the county hospital was boring and meaningless; after a few weeks I refused to go. Even my dream family was letting me down: it had grown up, but there seemed nowhere for it to go. The dream itself became a series of sentimental tragedies, like soap opera. I wrote the whole thing out, thinking I was writing a novel, but actually it was only therapy. I came to resent my father's having intervened in regard to the State Hospital. Maybe it could have helped me. (The therapist of my late twenties told me that my father may have saved me: the mere custodial care of state hospitals of that time could have made me worse and permanently ill.)

Looking back now, I see an entirely different picture. I see breaking point postponed until I was a student in a good hospital. And the father who had been virtually a stranger became a friend determined to make me well. He emerged as an instinctive therapist. He gave me jobs I could do in the office, and paid me. He encouraged my love of gardening and led me into a hiking club. I wanted to do a lot of reading and writing, and he supported me in doing this, often remarking that I was giving myself a good education. This stranger who became a friend also grew expressively affectionate, but this was so unfamiliar I could not reciprocate, only endure. He let me blow up at him, and sometimes exploded in return.

Even at the time I was affected by the transformation in my father. From an ingrown and absent-minded man, submerged in chronic financial worries, he became an outgoing, friendly, and caring person—not only in the family but in the community. He began doing new things and making new friends. He was, at the beginning of this sequence, fifty-five years old. And something in me knew that this change came about from the responsibility he took for me. When new life opened up for Thomas Kelly in his forties he said the cosmic mother lived in him. Maybe it was something like that for my father in regard to me, but it never occurred to us to talk about it.

A man I met in the hiking club started coming to the house. His name was Christian and he was a gentle and quiet person fifteen years older than I, and one of the few people I felt at home with at that time. He and my father became good friends. This man and I were two frightened people clinging to each other. As a foreigner who had lost his job in the early depression he was frightened at seeing his modest savings running out. I was afraid of a world where I had failed, and which had failed me. A year after we met we married and began to live with my family.

A very important discovery came to me toward the end of this first period of my life. I stumbled into Asian history, scriptures, and art. There, especially in Hinduism, I found confirmation of my temperament, a sense of worth which my own culture had not validated. My sense of self began to firm up. For the Hindu it seems more natural to live in the present than to become involved in the past and future. Mythic and mystical realities are more honored, and the distillation of intuitions into aphorisms is an engrained part of the culture. (Years later I heard a fellow staff member affectionately describe me as "strong in introvertive intuition because I was spilling aphorisms all over the place.")

At the age of twenty-four I was going to have a baby. I wanted that baby terribly. Chris, a master craftsman, had started a business making individual pieces of furniture. I was beginning to sell some writing here and there. My father was ecstatic about the coming baby. I never saw him so happy. Three months before the baby arrived he died of a heart attack.

The last time I saw him I blew up at him with savage anger, and he responded in kind. Interestingly, I did not feel guilt about this after he died, partly because I felt I was justified, and partly because I saw the whole scene as symbolizing a deep unresolved area of our relationship. Ten more years were to pass before I could even begin to forgive him for having withdrawn his attention from the little girl that I was. I could not even have put my finger on this at the time. (His one really great relation to his growing children was his love of *Alice in Wonderland,* which he read to us every year.) As I grew older I came to see that my introversion, which he found so disturbing, related to his own introversion, discredited by an extroverted culture.

## 2. *The Courage to Change*

Life now became a gradual trusting of unfamiliar states of mind. True, I had periods of bad depression, and so did Chris. I worked at poorly paid journalism during those years; both of us were impractical in financial matters. It amazes me how we managed to raise two children.

Many people we knew idealized the "simple life" as Chris and I appeared to symbolize it—something I didn't know until someone told me years later. But the joke was on them, for we didn't know how to do otherwise. Being slim earners doesn't necessarily make life simple. But from knowing people with more money—some of whom could be called rich—I realized we didn't have any more problems than the others. I had no illusions as to what money could do, short of relieving grinding poverty. As one Quaker said, "The Bloms live on a shoestring, but the shoestring is always long enough." Of course, it's easier to live on a shoestring if you're middle class and most people you know have more. Twice when economic disaster hit us the Quaker Meeting provided funds to carry us through.

When I first walked into the Friends Meeting of Chappaqua, New York, I said to myself, "I've come home for the first time in my life." Quakerism, with all its weaknesses and flaws, turned out to be an extended family and a homeland. At the time I wasn't sure whether I was a Hindu or Buddhist, and I had no relation to Christianity. When I wondered aloud about this a year later I was told, "You belong with us." My homeland in the Society of Friends opened many things for me. I was part of a group that built a Peace Forum in our area and a consumer cooperative store. I joined the Fellowship of Reconciliation and became involved in inter-racial activity. Before and during World War II Chris and I took in an occasional refugee from Nazi Germany for a rest or vacation. Later we shared important holidays with people from far places, contacted through the American Friends Service Committee.

When I first joined my Quaker Meeting I was the only member under fifty, and I was half that age. Now when I go back to that meeting I see new faces—young singles and young families. The whole Quarterly Meeting (Purchase Quarter in Westchester County, New York, and southern Connecticut) has discovered explosive new life and expansion since the 1930's, when it seemed to be dying out.

During the early days of the Peace Forum the American Friends Service Committee sent us an education team for the summer. Since I was handling publicity for the Forum I worked closely with one member of that team. For the first time in my life I fell in love, and found being in love terribly alive with both joy and pain. We shared and cared deeply, but never discussed this central matter. Not till many years later did we even hint at what the relationship had meant. I fell in love again in my late thirties—with a man much like my father who actually helped me to understand my father. Both times I felt incapable of breaking my marriage, and I didn't think I could endure my marriage if I developed a sexual relationship outside of it. I have come to realize since then how idealized this kind of love can be, because it never gets tested by the grinding-fine of years of everyday domestic problems. Falling in love is one way of discovering how alive one is, and I agree with Harold Goddard of Swarthmore that it provides a hint of the possibility of falling in love with life. The experiences of falling in love seem to be "educational toys," and it takes all we've got to learn from them.

Our family life was rough. Each step my husband or I took tended to lead us away from each other. Both of us continued to have periodic depressions. I felt I had never been a child and didn't know how to communicate with children. Chris was a fine father when our offspring were young, but as they began to emerge as complex persons, he was no better than I. For me the raising of children was like climbing the hard stone steps of necessity—maybe a necessity that held me together. Under the circumstances, the children had many problems that were painful both for them and for us. As adults both of them, in their very different ways, have transcended a great deal over the years, finding their own separate and very different paths. Chris knew I needed change more than he, and helped make it possible for me to have a few days respite at Pendle Hill at intervals.

Fritz Kunkel, a religiously oriented psychiatrist whose book, *Creation Continues,* helped me find my own relation to the Bible, once told a group at Pendle Hill that the greatest gift a parent can give a child is the testimony of his or her continuing growth, even if this shows up only when the child has become an adult. Maybe this is the most important thing my children have had from their family—a sense of life process.

During this period I continued to write, did a little lecturing, and followed my love of learning where it guided me. As for my spiritual life, the most significant landmark for those decades was Gerald Heard. I discovered him in 1939, and through him the Vedanta Society. I then followed him as he rediscovered his own roots in the Bible, of which he tells us in *The Creed of Christ* and *The Code of Christ*. Before entering the religious field he had been a science reporter on radio in England. Howard Brinton, also a great influence on me during my years at Pendle Hill, had been a physicist before moving on to the study of Quakerism. People who move comfortably between science and religion, finding a relationship between the two, appeal to me.

I was twenty-eight when I read Heard's *Pain, Sex, and Time,* a survey of Western history based on changing relations to these three elements in the culture. The book also gave me my first awareness of the way in which the physical being often reacts to emotional and spiritual conditions. I had an assortment of chronic and intermittent physical disorders in my young years which gradually disappeared. Even now I often learn from such disorders, and they usually disappear as I learn. Gerald Heard has said that most illness reflects other problems, and over the years more and more medical doctors have come to agree with him.

In *Pain, Sex, and Time* he concluded that we and our world can't change significantly unless we make time every day for meditation. I began getting up an hour before the children to meditate. Out of this meditation, after a few months, came my first religious experience since I was a child.

It is impossible to describe that experience. I can only express it in terms of "as if. . . ." Ever since, I've thought of it as if God had lifted me to a mountain top, giving me an overall view of creation, and then lowered me again. As I entered the bustle of the day I experienced light-headedness, as from breathing too rarified air, and found this more and more disconcerting as the hours passed. I began to long for the old familiar ballast of anxiety and tensions. But I need not have worried: before the day was out my "familiar self" returned.

As for the whole experience, it was as if God said to me: "This is your mountain. You are at its base, ready to climb.

Oil on canvas

NATIONAL GALLERY OF ART
WASHINGTON, D.C.

*THE MEETING OF SAINT ANTHONY AND SAINT PAUL: Sasseta (Sienese, 1392-1450). "Of all paintings," writes the author, "this comes most often to my mind as representing the life journey, moving from one position to another in relation to self, world, and God. Here it divides into three stages, as in my own life."*

Whether you ever reach the top again or not, you will always be on this mountain. Often you will lose the view, even lose the path, and you will often find it rocky and steep. How can you move to higher ground without sometimes losing the view and finding the going rough? But never forget: this is your mountain and you will always be on it."

I have never forgotten, and the mountain has become my strongest symbol of life journey, as the Tree of Life has been for the "self." The Sienese artist, Sassetta, gave me another relation to mountain as life journey with his *Meeting of St. Anthony and St. Paul.* Here is an image of movement in and out of the woods upon the mountain, and on the way down a meeting with a mythic creature (a link between heaven and earth perhaps), and a return to the world of human relationships—even as Christ withdrew to make fresh contact with God, and later returned.

I have never completely forsaken daily meditation, even though there have been long dry periods and many half-hearted ones, with sometimes a temptation to waste energy berating myself for not having made more progress up the mountain!

In my early forties my mother had an accident that led to great changes in both our lives. We were strangers, she and I, incomprehensible to each other, even though we managed to co-author a number of books. We shared the same house and it worked well, because her job required traveling most of the time. Then she fell, breaking her hip. Following an operation, she came home to spend many months in a wheel chair, confined and isolated in the house with me. It was rugged for both of us. Chris was closer to her than I was, and without his coming and going the situation would have been unthinkable.

Still, there were little miracles along the way. She had always hated her mother. Later I learned from a childhood friend of hers that her mother was an alcoholic who hated this daughter, and seriously abused her. After months in a wheel chair, my mother said, "I've been thinking a lot about my mother, realizing what a lonely and unhappy person she was." She spoke tenderly. Following this miracle of forgiveness she grew able to express and receive affection. Formerly this was possible for her only with babies. From then on, she and I had occasional moments of deep sharing and tenderness.

As the long winter wore on we both became depressed. Sometimes I managed a day off, and as was my custom on days off, I went into New York to a museum. Once, as I moved around the Metropolitan Museum, I found myself in an isolating fog, and couldn't make real contact with any of the art. I resigned myself to simply floating from gallery to gallery. Suddenly I was standing before a painting with tears of joy streaming down my face. Floods of compassion welled up from within me and flowed around me. The painting was a small head of Christ by Rembrandt. I had never noticed it before.

When I left the museum the whole world looked different, everything and everybody. Even strangers on the street were lovable—not from my love, but from a love coming through me. For about three weeks this new seeing persisted and then began to fade, leaving me not where it found me but in a new place, both within myself and in relation to the world.

When I try to understand how and why this event with the Christ picture happened, I see it as coming from the depth of my need (which I was well aware of), and at the same time from the inner space, the emptiness, which provided room for something new to happen. Was it, perhaps, a realization of the first Beatitude: Blessed are the poor in spirit, for theirs is the kingdom of heaven?

## III. *Continuing Creation*

I knew I must change my life, as truly as did Rilke when, in concluding his "Archaic Torso of Apollo," he wrote, "for there is no place/ that does not see you. You must change your life." The writing I'd been doing had come to a dead end. It drained my creative ability without being creative. I knew I must explore the function of art as it heals and transforms. A lot of things needed sorting out, and I didn't know how to start.

One day in early spring I walked up the second important

Oil on canvas

METROPOLITAN MUSEUM OF ART
MR. AND MRS. ISAAC D. FLETCHER COLLECTION
BEQUEST OF ISAAC D. FLETCHER, 1917

*HEAD OF CHRIST: Rembrandt Hermensz van Ryn (Dutch, 1606-69). At a time of great need this painting awakened in the author a new relation to life that led to a fresh beginning. It launched her on the second half of life which, for some of us, is the better half.*

forest road of my life. It took me to a hilltop crowned with an open field, symbolically bringing together the woods and field that had been separated in the childhood experience. I threw myself down in the early spring sun. I felt the heartbeat of the earth, perhaps a thousand insects beneath the surface awakening in response to new warmth. The sky hovered close. I felt embraced and loved, and minutes passed. I knew myself born of a new consummation in the marriage of Heaven and Earth. At that moment I discovered Mother Earth and Father Spirit as my parents, freeing my biological parents to be fallible, fumbling, well-intentioned human beings like me. Truly this was one of the liberating moments of my life. This freeing of parents in adulthood may be one of the most important happenings to people in our culture.

The experience released new energy to explore "what next." I looked for and found a half-time job in a store where I worked three days a week, first selling, later decorating windows, arranging displays, and assisting the buyer. I worked there twelve years, slowly tapering down the time as I built a new career. That store was a challenge to my weak areas; to meet the challenge was an essential part of becoming whole. My job demanded that I be less absent-minded, work matter-of-factly with merchandize that was uninteresting, handle money and keep records accurately. Hardest of all, it demanded that I relate to people on a superficial basis for hours at a time. I was just discovering Buber's "I and Thou," and often tried to make room for this "event" as described by Buber. There were some impressive results, as with arrogant and demanding customers who were not used to service people being totally present and caring. I tried to honor the need that made them that way, at the same time listening intently and searchingly for something more real within them. Invariably such a person would become like a sweet little child as the thorny, protective crust crumbled. It made me see what a mask crustiness is: often it obscures a little child who never grew up. Actually, the experience of that job which I never would have chosen increased my confidence in myself immeasurably.

The rest of the week I spent on my own custom-made education, and in the pursuit of my question: what is the inherent function of art? Within two years I came to several conclusions. First, art at its best is a by-product of religious experience, a non-verbal language which communicates with non-verbal parts of ourselves. Secondly, every culture, every period, every true artist educates us to a different relation to reality. For art has the power, when allowed, to transform both inner and outer reality. The art imagery we focus on most, by circumstance or by choice, forms the value system we live by.

Books by writers who trust these things—Elie Faure, Malraux, Paul Tillich, Clive Bell, Evelyn Underhill, Jacques Maritain, Sorokin, the late works of Herbert Read, and even Whitehead—are not usually included in art school and college courses. This venture of mine into the function of art took place in the early 1950's, and the books I valued most belonged to a period ranging from 1915 to the time of my search. Some have become classics. Now one can find certain popular priced books where art and the religious approach to life are no longer separated, but much harder to find are those where cultural assumptions and personal value systems are affected by art.

After two years I began teaching in adult schools and doing a little lecturing and seminar work. This teaching can be described as arising from a place where art, religion and growth processes converge within the context of our changing world. Teaching, along with royalties from earlier writing, made it possible to help my children with their education.

A whole new life was opening for me during my forties. Yet increasingly I felt a "possession," an irrational fixation I could not get rid of. A friend suggested I see Martha Jaeger, a Jungian therapist in New York, a Quaker who worked with many artists. Martha became my therapist and teacher for two years, training me in growth processes, both for my own needs and for working with others, as I found myself more and more consulted by members of my Meeting and my students. Martha and I remained very close friends until her death.

As for the possession, Martha saw it as the healthy assertion of my weakest endowment. This was my sensation function, in Jung's terminology. Exploring this, we saw clearly that my sense experiences had a hard time holding their own against the tides of feeling that swamped them. (A friend once told me I was the only person she knew who could sit in an uncomfortable position and not notice.) The Puritanical West, of course, honored the conceptual rather than fresh, new sense experience. The relation to the senses had become ambiguous, associated with the merely sensual person, where the senses had taken over in place of wholeness.

Martha insisted my relation to the senses affected my relation to myself as artist and might explain why I left the artist in me behind, years ago. To function well, she said, the artist depends upon fresh new sense experience where the whole person is gathered to receive the new impression. (It sounded like Buber's *I and Thou.*) She taught me to hold emotion back until a sensation could realize itself in its own right. If the artist in me was not starved to death, at least she was weak from undernourishment and neglect. One of the new beginnings of my forties was rediscovering this artist in me, coming to find its function, seeing it as an essential part of my being, needing to serve my relation to God, others, and myself. As I ventured into making more room for vital new impressions the artist in me responded with eagerness.

One summer I made pinch pots with Paulus Berensohn at Pendle Hill. When I went home I asked a student of mine, Eloise Harmon, a fine sculptor whose medium is clay, where to go to learn more about clay. She had just lost her apprentice, and asked if I would serve as replacement a couple of half-days a week. This meant earning while learning; apprenticeship is the best education of all. Of course I would! I found working in three dimensions exhilarating. Within a couple of years I showed a few pieces at art fairs and shops, selling some.

In clay I missed working in color (the outer equivalent of feeling, my strongest endowment of temperament). If clay was a gift given me in my forties, free stitchery, revelling in colored yarns, was the gift of my fifties. In my sixties the gift was water color as meditation. All this proved to me that the creative faculty never gets lost, even when ignored for twenty years as mine was. Surely Hugh Mearns was right in saying, after experience with old people, that everyone has the creative faculty, and one can discover it and use it at any age: it doesn't deteriorate.

But teaching remained my first art. I was teaching three sections of the same class each week, with most students returning year after year and getting to know each other well. Together we focused on the art of many periods and many cultures, learning to communicate with the aspects of human nature and the value systems involved, each member adding personal discovery to the group experience. Some used to refer to classes as "spiritual growth groups." There were always several Friends in the classes, and through them, Quakerism began to find the approach relevant to itself. As far as the Pleasantville Adult classes were concerned, I never could repeat a course in sixteen years because so many students continued year after year. Martha Jaeger once said those classes were a better education than I could buy, because I always had to be a step ahead of the students.

In many ways these were good years. The children were moving off in their own directions, and Chris and I developed a relationship which became simpler and more deliberately supportive of each other in our very different interests and needs. His were sports, music, languages (he spoke seven, including his native Afrikaans) and most of all being the master craftsman he was. In a way Chris and I became best friends, caring very much how each other felt.

During the late 1950's Chris suffered alarming symptoms, finally diagnosed as emphysema. For the last ten years of his life he was increasingly a semi-invalid, but managed to work a few hours a day. During the last few months before he died he was severely depressed, as if weary of carrying the illness and fearing a time he could no longer work. He died of a heart attack, by his work bench, after dragging a fallen cripple from the railroad track next to his shop.

Strangely, he died close to the day, a year later, that a younger sister of mine died. This and other similarities made the events mythic, or like a Greek chorus. Both deaths were sudden and unexpected. Both times someone said to me (in effect), "Come quick! Something is the matter with. . . ." Each time I went and knew immediately that the other was not living and said: "Go get a doctor. I'll stay here." And each time I held the body in my arms, acutely aware of it giving me its last body heat. Instead of shock or realization (which came later) I felt calm closeness, a sense of standing together at a portal. These two had each left behind a life that had become, for different reasons, an unbearable weight.

This presentness in death with those with whom I had shared much life was surely awesome, affecting deeply my relation to death. Life endures, perhaps, because we tend mostly to shun and even abhor death. Otherwise human life might not have survived on this earth. But during the second half of life it seems important to confront death again and again in such a way that we can gradually make friends with it. This may come easier for me because of the intimate experience with those two family deaths.

The day before Chris died he may have had the first mystical experience of our life together. That afternoon I asked him a question regarding his preference about something. In response to his answer I did the opposite. He burst into an explosion of temper. Deliberately, with calculation, I answered in kind, shouting, "After all these years can't you accept my absent-mindedness? Look what you're doing, spending your precious energy on such a little thing!" Maybe because I hadn't shouted at him angrily in a long time it shocked him. He sat there in silence, seemingly brow-beaten—small, fragile, spent. Then suddenly, as if he heard a sound, he looked up into the far corner of the room, alert, strong, in rapt attention. A few seconds? A minute? Timeless. Finally his face relaxed into a slight smile. Obviously he did not want to talk: he opened a book and began to read.

A younger woman in my Friends Meeting said to me, "When a person you've lived closely with for a long time dies, that person has finished dying, but life as you have known it takes a year to die." For one thing, I soon noticed how the psychological space had changed: people do inhabit and affect space, and if suddenly their presence is withdrawn there is an unfamiliar climate.

The same person told me to notice the gifts of the dead, and I did—all the way from a gathering of many who had been important in our thirty-five years of married life, yet had never been gathered together at one time, to the idea for a memorial in the form of a Black African book collection in our public library. Chris was from South Africa, grew up on a tenant farm playing with native children, speaking their language, knowing their stories, and singing their songs. He did not leave Africa until he was thirty. One of the happiest events of his later years was his visit, through Martha Jaeger, with Laurens Van der Post when the latter was in New York.

Perhaps another gift of the dead was the awareness of how many times we'd let each other down during our years of marriage—of the problems needing resolution, plus the insight to handle them. Both of us, I felt, needed to forgive and be forgiven. I knew I must never think of his need or mine separately without recalling the other. I must experience them simultaneously. By the end of a year I had a profound sense of mutual forgiveness. William Blake wrote:

> And so, throughout eternity,
> I forgive you, you forgive me. . . .

Of one thing I am sure: important life relationships do continue after death. I am not interested in speculating on the metaphysical and parapsychological aspects of this (although I suspect that in some incomprehensible way such experiences are a two-way matter), but I well know my own experience of it. Even now, twelve years later, I dream of Chris twice a year, and I'm always amazed at what is obviously a further stage in the development of our relationship.

The year after Chris died Joe and Teresina Havens, Friends on sabbatical in London, teased me into spending some time with them. My son bought me an air ticket, and I who never thought to travel, who claimed, rather, that the world came to me, discovered a new beginning. As a part of that first trip the Havens arranged a seminar for me to do in London, sponsored by three Quaker organizations and climaxed by an open lecture at the Tate Gallery. From then on I found myself, from time to time, doing programs in far places. Also, I received two gift trips: one to Italy from Pleasantville Adult School students, and one to India from students and co-workers at Pendle Hill.

As an older single I have not only a vocation which affords me challenge and livelihood, but also a religious family. These two things I would wish for older singles everywhere.

Quakerism does not necessarily provide a better family or homeland than others. I am in great debt to other religious groups, as well as having spiritual relatives among them. But Quakerism is where *I* belong, supplying me with a long range continuity through which I have struggled, grown, suffered, and rejoiced. For me it is my spiritual laboratory in which I have tested truth, relationship, and vision in this unfamiliar world.

During the 1960's my growing spiritual relation to art led to widening circles within Quakerism and other groups. (Now I go only to places where I already have continuity, since the relational has high priority for me.) Three years after Chris died I responded to Pendle Hill's request that I be a guest teacher for one year—and I stayed six.

There I found the most amazing groups of people I have ever known. Each year a new student body gathers, adults ranging from twenty to eighty years old. They come together to spend eight months taking a new look at life—not for credits or prestige, but to know themselves and life in a new depth of understanding. For some the decision to come costs risk and sacrifice. These groups contain Protestants, Jews, Catholics, Quakers, and sometimes one or more Hindus or Buddhists to fill out the picture. It's hard for me to imagine living in this situation without accelerating growth, or without—almost invariably—some measure of pain as a part of the process.

Of the many by-products of those years I share one incident that became an important release for me. I had a student who attended two sections of one of my classes at Pendle Hill because he was afraid he "might miss something," and therefore had no fear of hurting my feelings. He often stayed to talk after the second class as I took down the pictures. We came to know each other well. Once, when I impatiently mentioned a small, inconvenient handicap I had, he burst out, "Dorothea, you're a dyslexic, didn't you know? My mother runs a school for them, and I tutored them in college, so I know one when I see one." "What's a dyslexic?" I asked. He rolled off a number of things: slow reader, non-speller, not knowing left from right, poor visual motor control, etc., then concluded, "It's okay! Dyslexics tend to be very creative. Einstein was one." I burst out laughing. I felt like the boy whose parents always avoided reference to his harelip. When he heard someone refer to him as "the boy with the harelip" he ran to his mother in great excitement exclaiming, "Now I know what it is. It's got a name! It's called a harelip."

I was sixty when that happened, and I still enjoy laughing over the incident and its effect on me. Laughter heals. In fact, I consider laughter the lubricant that makes life possible. You can't drive a car on lubricant alone, but don't try driving without it.

Now, even as I notice an aging process slowly proceeding (*growing* old is my intention, not *getting* old), I often feel younger than when I was young, physically healthier and more playful. Growing old is not easy (maybe life never is), but for me it's easier than growing up or being young. As for humor (which I originally learned from my husband), finding it in many things is increasingly a part of it all—big and little things, trivial and serious things, alone and with others!

From Pendle Hill I moved on to another adult learning and retreat center, Koinonia Foundation in Baltimore—another place which is changing in response to a changing world. I have already started my fifth year there. Pendle Hill and Koinonia have a good relationship, sometimes serving each other as a place of retreat for staff when needed.

Both centers have been willing to release me for short term teaching at Woodbrooke, the British institution which inspired Pendle Hill, Vittakivi in Finland, which was inspired *by* Pendle Hill, and other places—including two periods of teaching in a Catholic Christian Brothers Novitiate for young men!

About a quarter of the staff of Koinonia is Quaker. Early in 1978 Richard Falkenstein and I started the Koinonia Friends Meeting. During the first couple of months Dick and I were the only attenders, but by spring there were several of us regularly, residents and non-residents, and now it looks as if it's here to stay.

These years have made of me a bit of a connoisseur of group living in adult learning and retreat centers. As a staff person I find such centers exciting, intense, and at times exhausting. The interaction tends to grind off sharp corners and rough spots for all concerned. We sometimes recognize little miracles happening to one another, whether we are staff, students, or retreatants. Even as I made brief visits to Pendle Hill many times in earlier years, so do persons return again and again to similar places for renewal. Each, for many people, becomes a "Mecca with blemishes," as I used to call Pendle Hill. All go through periods of boat rocking, including the Aurobindo Ashram in India: maybe it's the nature of the beast. In this catapulting world of ours, where the boat never rocks there may be no life.

A word which has meant much during this decade is "convergence," adapted from Teilhard de Chardin. Through it I find aspects of myself discovering one another, just as various cultures feed renewal into one another, without any one of them forfeiting its own uniqueness. This culminates in the impulse toward organic wholeness of life, though there is a basic danger, perhaps, in the fear bred by the unfamiliar and by change itself both in ourselves and in the world, which drives many persons and groups to violence in attitude or action.

Teilhard says the center of the universe is where a person is, and that God is the Center of centers. When these two come together the way opens, as at a crossroad, in all directions. For me this awakens a mandala image which I have painted, on three occasions, as a water color meditation. Only through the center, detached from particulars, can we see in all directions, recognizing values that need salvaging. The mandala, with its center and related parts, is the ideal tool in an age of monumental convergence. Why else has this archetypal form become reborn for us? We encounter it in many cultures and among the masters of the twentieth century. Chagall's "Benjamin Window" gives us a truly kinetic mandala—process itself—with peripheral figuration. In some inexplicable way it has taught me what Heaven is: a fifth dimension, encompassing and containing all lesser dimensions.

As my religion, art, and growth processes interact with this enormous rocking boat—the planet we share—the whole matter of myself as Friend and artist increasingly becomes another convergence in my life. The three Quaker beliefs that have underscored this convergence are simplicity, that of God in everyone, and continuing revelation.

As for simplicity, the artist in me wants to simplify, to choose what rings true, and to slough off what gets in the way, while I think of that of God in everyone as the creative aspect of human nature, made in God's image, giving our species the capacity to choose involvement in continuing creation. When we experience something of God within us we know more of human nature. And maybe it's "that of God" in the human organism that makes possible continuing revelation. In a discussion group at Woodbrooke the leader expressed gratitude for my having used the term "continuing revelation," which he called the most neglected of the Quaker testimonies. This shocked me, because for me continuing revelation is the essential partner of continuing creation which, though not a stated

Marble  
Photograph courtesy of Phaidon Press

ACCADEMIA DI BELLE ARTI  
FLORENCE

*THE CAPTIVE ATLAS: Michelangelo Buonarroti (Florentine, 1475-1564). Long known as one of the "unfinished statues" of the Boboli Gardens, this powerful art image reveals the struggle to pull oneself loose from the habits and attitudes that stand in the way of finding one's own shape.*

testimony, is implicit in the recognized testimonies. And art at its best, whether mine or another's, is part of continuing revelation. The very concept of life journey, moving to new positions in relation to self and to life, depends upon it. Desirable social change is inconceivable without it.

Habitual, mechanical patterns of thought and action are the real enemies of revelation. And for me, living with strong imagery through reproductions and art books is an enormous help in freeing me from dead habit, and even *idealistic rigidities,* to make room for revelation. My favorites for this purpose have been Michelangelo's so-called "Unfinished Statues" in the Accademia in Florence. These figures seem to be pulling themselves out of bedrock—we could say "deadrock"—to find each its own shape, one capable of containing needed new vision.

Revelation sometimes comes to us in spite of ourselves, whether we can make good use of it or not. But it seems that we are most open to it when we don't "know" the answers. It takes courage to trust the unknown—Mystery itself—out of which revelation comes. I think of it as learning not to be afraid of the dark, even to love the dark, *and* to be loved by it. Sometimes, for me, the Christ figure stands in for Mystery, walking on the troubled waters of our world or of my troubled spirit, or leaping from the Cross to bless us.

Maybe my greatest miracle of convergence is my relation to my own culture. If, when young, I felt either the culture or I had to be wrong, now I know that I and my culture are two sides of life needing each other. Because I am more Hindu than Western by temperament, I well knew the weakness of its one-sidedness even before I went to India. I know, too, the weakness and dangers of the one-sided Western culture, especially in its extreme form in the United States. Yes, I know these things with my whole being: my culture needs the likes of me if it is to survive, just as I need my culture to be healthy and whole. We are both dangerously incomplete, maybe obsolete, without each other.